The Last Will and Testament
of an Extremely Distinguished Dog

No matter how

deep my *sleep*

I shall hear

you and not all

the *power* of

death can keep

my *spirit* from

wagging a

grateful *tail*.

Eugene O'Neill

THE LAST WILL AND TESTAMENT OF AN EXTREMELY DISTINGUISHED

Dog

AMERICAN ROOTS

Applewood Books
CARLISLE, MASSACHUSETTS

978-1-4290-9607-2

Cover art © 2014 Michael Halbert
Interior art © 2014 Noble Illustrations

"The Last Will and Testament of a Distinguished Dog" was originally written on December 17, 1940. The work was written at Tao House, located in Danville, California, the Monterey Colonial hillside home of America's only Nobel Prize-winning playwright, Eugene O'Neill.

Thank you for purchasing an Applewood book.
Applewood reprints America's lively classics—
books from the past that are still of interest to modern readers.
Our mission is to build a picture of America's
past through its primary sources.

To inquire about this edition or to request a free copy of
our current catalog featuring our best-selling books, write to:
Applewood Books
P.O. Box 27
Carlisle, MA 01741
For more complete listings, visit us on the web at www.awb.com

10 9 8 7 6

MANUFACTURED IN THE UNITED STATES OF AMERICA

The short works Applewood offers in its American Roots series have been selected to connect us. The books are tactile mementos of American passions by some of America's most famous writers. Each of these has meant something very personal to me.

After our first dog, Cadie, who lived to be nineteen, died, it took a long time for my wife and I to bring another dog into our lives. Cadie was smart and active, protective and loyal, but mostly she was our beloved first child. My wife adopted her when we were in college. Cadie lived nineteen years before my two young boys and I, connected by phone with my wife at work, listened to Cadie take her last breaths on the floor of our bedroom. There would never be another like her; she was my wife's other soul-mate. I wish I had found this beautiful message from Blemie to share with my wife. It would have been salve for both our hurts.

> *"No matter how deep my sleep I shall hear you and not all the power of death can keep my spirit from wagging a grateful tail."*

                          ❧Phil Zuckerman

                              PUBLISHER

I Silverdene Emblem O'Neill (familiarly known to my family, friends & acquaintances as Blemie), because the burden of my years and infirmities is heavy upon me, and I realize the end of my life is near, do hereby bury my last will and testament in the mind of my Master. He will not know it is there until after I am dead. Then, remembering me in his loneliness, he will suddenly know of this testament, and I ask him then to inscribe it as a memorial to me.

I have little in the way of material things to leave. Dogs are wiser than men. They do not set great store upon things. They do not waste their days hoarding property. They do not ruin their sleep worrying about how to keep the objects they have, and to obtain the objects they have not. There is nothing of value I have to bequeath except my love and my faith. These I leave to all those who have loved me, to my Master and Mistress, who I know will mourn me most, to Freeman who has been so good to me, to Cyn and Roy and Willie and Naomi and—But if I should list all those who have loved me, it would force my Master to write a book. Perhaps it is vain of me to boast when I am so near death, which returns all beasts and vanities to dust, but I have always been an extremely lovable dog.

I ask my Master and Mistress to remember me always, but not to grieve for me too long. In my life I have tried to be a comfort to them in time of sorrow, and a reason for added joy in their happiness. It is painful for me to think that even in death I should cause them pain. Let them remember that while no dog has ever had a happier life (and this I owe to their love and care for me), now that I have grown blind and deaf and lame, and even my sense of smell fails me so that a rabbit could be right under my nose and I might not know, my pride has sunk to a sick, bewildered humiliation. I feel life is taunting me with having over-lingered my welcome. It is time I said good-bye, before I become too sick a burden on myself and on those who love me. It will be sorrow to leave them, but not a sorrow to die. Dogs do not fear death as men do. We accept it as part of life, not as something alien and terrible which destroys life. What may come after death, who knows? I would like to believe with those of my fellow Dalmatians who are devout Mohammedans, that there is a Paradise where one is always young and full-bladdered; where all the day one dillies and dallies with an amorous multitude of houris, beautifully spotted; where jack rabbits that run fast but not too fast (like the houris) are as the sands of the desert; where each blissful hour is mealtime; where in long evenings there are a million fireplaces with logs forever burning, and one curls oneself up and blinks into the flames and nods and dreams, remembering the old brave days on earth, and the love of one's Master and Mistress.

I am afraid this is too much for even such a dog as I am to expect. But peace, at least, is certain. Peace and long rest for weary old heart and head and limbs, and eternal sleep in the earth I have loved so well. Perhaps, after all, this is best.

One last request I earnestly make. I have heard my Mistress say, "When Blemie dies we must never have another dog. I love him so much I could never love another one." Now I would ask her, for love of me, to have another. It would be a poor tribute to my memory never to have a dog again. What I would like to feel is that, having once had me in the family, now she cannot live without a dog! I have never had a narrow jealous spirit. I have always held that most dogs are good (and one cat, the black one I have permitted to share the living room rug during the evenings, whose affection I have tolerated in a kindly spirit, and in rare sentimental moods, even reciprocated a trifle). Some dogs, of course, are better than others. Dalmatians, naturally, as everyone knows, are best. So I suggest a Dalmatian as my successor. He can hardly be as well bred or as well mannered or as distinguished and handsome as I was in my prime. My Master and Mistress must not ask the impossible. But he will do his best, I am sure, and even his inevitable defects will help by comparison to keep my memory green. To him I bequeath my collar and leash and my overcoat and raincoat, made to order in 1929 at Hermes in Paris. He can never wear them with the distinction I did, walking around the Place Vendôme, or later along Park Avenue, all eyes fixed on me in admiration; but again I am sure he will do his utmost not to appear a mere gauche provincial dog. Here on the ranch, he may prove himself quite worthy of comparison, in some respects. He will, I presume, come closer to jack rabbits than I have been able to in recent years. And for all his faults, I hereby wish him the happiness I know will be his in my old home.

One last word of farewell, Dear Master and Mistress. Whenever you visit my grave, say to yourselves with regret but also with happiness in your hearts at the remembrance of my long happy life with you: "Here lies one who loved us and whom we loved." No matter how deep my sleep I shall hear you, and not all the power of death can keep my spirit from wagging a grateful tail.

TAO HOUSE,
DECEMBER 17TH, 1940

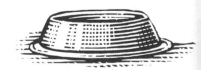